A Kids' Guide to
Helping Others
Read & Succeed

How to Take Action!

Cathryn Berger Kaye, M.A.

free spirit
PUBLiSHiNG®

Helping kids
help themselves™
since 1983

Library of Congress Cataloging-in-Publication Data
Kaye, Cathryn Berger.
    A kids' guide to helping others read and succeed : how to take action / by Cathryn Berger Kaye.
        p. cm.
    ISBN-13: 978-1-57542-241-1
    ISBN-10: 1-57542-241-7
    1. Language arts—Juvenile literature. 2. Social action—Juvenile literature. 3. Service learning—Juvenile literature. 4. Young volunteers in social service—Juvenile literature. I. Title.
    LB1576.K374 2007
    372.6—dc22
                                           2006102563

Service learning occurs in each of the fifty United States and internationally. Some project descriptions are attributed to specific schools or youth groups and identified by city, state, or region. All efforts have been made to ensure correct attribution. The names of the young people quoted throughout the book have been changed to protect their privacy.

The excerpt on pages 22–23 is from *Dear Whiskers* by Ann Whitehead Nagda (Holiday House, 2000). Reprinted with permission of Holiday House, Inc. Copyright © 2000 by Ann Whitehead Nagda.

Edited by Rebecca Aldridge and Meg Bratsch
Interior design by Jayne Curtis
Cover design by Marieka Heinlen

10 9 8 7 6 5 4 3 2 1
Printed in the United States of America

Free Spirit Publishing Inc.
217 Fifth Avenue North, Suite 200
Minneapolis, MN 55401-1299
(612) 338-2068
help4kids@freespirit.com
www.freespirit.com

Free Spirit Publishing is a member of the Green Press Initiative, and we're committed to printing our books on recycled paper containing a minimum of 30% post-consumer waste (PCW). For every ton of books printed on 30% PCW recycled paper, we save 5.1 trees, 2,100 gallons of water, 114 gallons of oil, 18 pounds of air pollution, 1,230 kilowatt hours of energy, and .9 cubic yards of landfill space. At Free Spirit it's our goal to nurture not only young people, but nature too!

Printed on recycled paper
including 30%
post-consumer waste

Acknowledgments
As always, the "village" concept comes into play with any service learning publication. To the many service learning colleagues who share stories and examples—thank you! To the youth who demonstrate dedication and passion—your ideas and vision inspire us all. To all at Free Spirit Publishing who contribute in myriad ways to the service learning field—hooray! And to my family who provides unconditional support and love—my heart is most grateful.

What's Inside

What Kids Think
of Working to Help Others
Read & Succeed

"We want our voices to be heard and to make change in the community. Sometimes adults underestimate us. But once they find out what we can do, they change their minds."
—Amber, age 13

"Would I do this again? Definitely. I would do another service learning project. Now I have even more ideas and probably more confidence."
—Lucas, age 16

"I spent more time on this book writing project than any other assignment. And I just love how it came out. We're making so many copies to give out. For the first time, I feel like an author!" —Natasha, age 12

"The entire class really pitched in. We worked together better than on any other project. I got to take photos, and I have always wanted to do that."
—Andy, age 13

"I didn't realize that everything could be related. I discovered that I was part of the bigger picture and that my words could have an impact on other people." —Drew, age 13

"Service changes everybody: The people doing the service, the people receiving the service, and the witnesses around. Everyone can be touched and everyone makes a difference." —Kira, age 15

"Every time I went to the after-school program to read to the kids, one little girl always climbed on my lap. At first I was only going to go three times. I decided to keep going every week for the rest of the semester."
—Ariel, age 14

The Wonder of Words

Can you imagine a world without words? How would you order popcorn at a movie? Write a happy birthday message on a card? Sing a favorite song? Send a text message to your friends? Tell a story?

To get an idea of how this might feel, try an activity. Find a partner and take turns trying to do the following things *without* using words (if you are working alone, try to communicate these things on a piece of paper *without* using words).

Describe the weather outside.

Detail what the inside of your home looks like.

Explain what you did yesterday when you got home from school.

Summarize your favorite movie and explain the reasons why you like it so much.

Now imagine you had to communicate like this all day, every day. It's pretty obvious the world needs words.

Literacy is a term commonly used to describe the ability to read, write, and understand words. It also often is used to describe a person's ability to work with numbers (*math literacy*) and to use a computer (*computer literacy*). Overall, literacy involves a process of learning that enables people to succeed, develop their knowledge and potential, and participate fully in society. You can bring literacy to life for others through service learning. This book will serve as your guide.

"To make a difference is not a matter of accident . . . people choose to make a difference."
—Maya Angelou, author

Starting Now

The following chapters will help you think of various ways to contribute to the literacy of others. Read the ideas below, and circle the ones you might like to do:

- Perform a play for kids to get them excited about reading.

- Write a book with a student who is just learning English about something you both like.

- Teach computer skills to an adult who has never used a computer.

- Help a younger student learn to count and do basic math.

- Collect books for kids and adults and put them in hospital waiting rooms.

- Start a library where none exists.

In this book you will read about similar ways kids around the world are getting involved in literacy projects. You will get a better idea of how service learning helps you identify your talents and skills and use them in creative ways to help others read and succeed. Whether you decide to work with an organization or start your own project, the time to start is now.

A Note About Using This Book

This guide is written for use by classes or youth groups, so the activity directions assume you are in a group of around 15 to 30 students. However, smaller groups, families, and individuals can easily adapt every activity. If you are using the book on your own, consider finding a friend to participate with you.

Tips for Using This Book

You are holding a written guide, but you will find other guides around you—adults you meet who are involved in service learning, friends and other students working with you, and community members who are eager to help.

✦ Keep track of your thoughts and observations in this book. Write in it whenever and wherever you want!

✦ You might also want to start your own service learning journal in a notebook.

✦ Share your ideas with others, no matter how far-fetched they may seem!

✦ Let your creativity inspire you.

Service + Learning = Service Learning

Service:
Service means contributing or helping to benefit others and the common good.

Learning:
Learning means gaining understanding of a subject or skill through study, instruction, or experience.

Service Learning:
The ideas of service and learning combine to create service learning. **Preparation, action, reflection,** and **demonstration** are the four stages of service learning. By understanding how these stages work, you can make plans more effectively to help in your community.

Following is an example of students involved in a literacy service learning project.

The TV-Turnoff Project

"How does watching TV affect literacy?" One class of middle school students decided to find out. A report they read said that each year American kids spend about 900 hours in school compared to 1,023 hours watching television. The students also did Internet research and interviewed a child psychologist. Through their research, they discovered that too much television viewing (four or more hours per day) hurt kids' reading and writing skills.

"I must say I find television very educational. The minute somebody turns it on, I go to the library and read a good book."
—Groucho Marx, actor

Next, the students joined a national program called TV-Turnoff Week and came up with project ideas to inspire other kids to join them. Participants kept a log of how many books they read during the week instead of watching television. Students collected and analyzed the data. They discovered everyone spent more time studying and reading for fun, which helped improve their literacy skills. As a final step, the class wrote an article for the local newspaper that included suggestions for how to spend TV-free time.

For information about TV-Turnoff Week, visit www.tvturnoff.org.

Stage 1: Preparation

In service learning, **preparation** involves getting background knowledge of your subject and coming up with ideas for action.

Which of these strategies did the students use to prepare for their TV-Turnoff project?

☐ research ☐ interviewing ☐ discussion ☐ brainstorming

Stage 2: Action

Once you are prepared with the background knowledge you need, you can create and carry out your **action** plan. Most often, you will take action in one or more of the following four ways.

Direct Service:
Your service involves face-to-face interactions with people, or close contact with them.

Indirect Service:
Your action is not seen by the people who may benefit from it, but it meets a real need.

Advocacy:
What you do makes others aware of an issue and encourages them to take action to change a situation.

Research:
You gather and report on information that helps a community.

In the TV-Turnoff project, students got others to join in TV-Turnoff Week (direct service), and gathered information about how many books kids read during the week (research). Then, they wrote a newspaper article to inform others of their findings (advocacy). An example of possible indirect service in this project would be creating a display in the school library featuring fun books to read instead of watching TV.

Which action category would each of the following activities fall under: direct service, indirect service, advocacy, or research? *Hint:* Some involve more than one type of action.

- Helping a child learn the alphabet
- Stocking bookshelves at a homeless shelter
- Designing a pamphlet on the importance of reading aloud to a child
- Leading a study skills workshop for students
- Creating board games that inspire interest in reading
- Writing a book about people in history who promoted education

Stage 3: Reflection

What is one piece of information you have learned so far that you want to remember?

....

What is one idea you now have that you didn't have before you opened this book?

....

When you answer these questions, you are participating in **reflection**: looking at your experience to determine what it has to do with you. Reflection takes place all along the way: as you prepare, as you do the service, and as you demonstrate what you have learned and accomplished. You will find reflection built into many of the activities in this book. When you see the Time for Reflection symbol, follow the directions to special reflection pages.

··· TIME FOR REFLECTION ⊒

Stage 4: Demonstration

Demonstration is the stage where you take the opportunity to let others know what you have learned and what good community work you have done. Are you an artist? Do you like to perform? Do you enjoy writing? Do you like taking photos? Are you a computer whiz? You could use any of these skills or talents to demonstrate your service learning. Circle ways you might want to **demonstrate** what you accomplish:

Make a mural.

Create a Web site.

Write an article for your school or community newspaper.

Build a display for a local library.

Put together a video or audio recording.

Perform a skit for another class or youth group.

Create a brochure showing the steps you followed.

Getting the Facts About Literacy

> "Literacy is not a luxury, it is a right and a responsibility."
> —Former U.S. President Bill Clinton

Nearly 100 percent of children in the United States and Europe attend school. Education encourages literacy. Literacy helps people gain knowledge, get jobs, and do daily things that may be taken for granted, like reading a job application, a sign in a store window, or a restaurant menu. Literacy skills also help people stay healthy and prevent disease. What are some ways that knowing how to read would help a person live a healthy life or keep others in their family healthy? Write your ideas here:

....

....

As you read the following facts, consider what each one means in the lives of real people.

FACT: More than 840 million adults in the world cannot read or write this sentence. They are **illiterate.**

FACT: Women who are **literate**—who have learned to read and write—are more likely to have smaller families with healthier, more educated children. But 538 million women in the world are illiterate.

FACT: 134 million children in the world between the ages of 7 and 18 have never been to school. An estimated 7 million children under the age of 14 are forced to work all day instead of go to school.

FACT: In many poor countries, only 5 percent of girls and 55 percent of boys attend school beyond the sixth grade. Without a basic education, they rarely have a chance to make a good living.

FACT: In the United States in 2006, many of the nation's largest public high schools had a dropout rate of over 60 percent of students.

What do these facts tell you about the challenges of achieving global literacy? Complete each of the following sentences with your own thoughts.

If children have to work instead of attending school, ...

....

Because children learn best in homes where parents can read, a community priority might be

....

....

A World View of Literacy

Travel the globe with the stories in this chapter to see the different ways literacy comes to life in all corners of the world.

Student Authors in Tanzania

Barbara Cervone is the director of a program called What Kids Can Do. Cervone has traveled to many parts of the world and has seen tremendous differences between what is and what is not available to help children learn. "In China," says Cervone, "I visited a school wired for computers way beyond what I have seen in the United States. And I have also spent extended time in a school in Kambi ya Simba, a remote village in Tanzania, where the only information available for students is what the teacher puts on the blackboard."

Every step of getting an education can be a struggle in Kambi ya Simba. Beyond sixth grade, a student must pay for school with cash and with part of his or her family's harvest, which the school uses for student meals. Often, 100 students fill one class. Yet even with all their challenges, the students of Kambi ya Simba are committed to learning and being global citizens.

As a project for their school and for What Kids Can Do, ten of the students, with adult guidance, collected the voices of 350 of their classmates through essays, videos, and interviews. The students also interviewed their parents and grandparents and took over a thousand photographs. They used the material to write a book—*In Our Village: Kambi ya Simba Through the Eyes of Its Youth*. Its 22 brief chapters show and tell how the people in their village respect the land, how they sing and dance, how they value friends and learning, and what they dream for the future. The book has been an amazing success, and students around the globe are creating similar books about their own communities to send to the students of Kambi ya Simba, creating a worldwide exchange of cultures.

To read an excerpt from *In Our Village* (Next Generation Press, 2006) and watch student-made videos, visit www.inourvillage.org. Click on "In Our Global Village" to find out how you can create a book about your community and send it to the students of Kambi ya Simba.

Imagine you are writing a book about the place where you live. What would be the titles of the first three chapters?

Chapter 1: ....

Chapter 2: ....

Chapter 3: ....

Share these chapter ideas with others to create a full table of contents for your own *In Our Global Village* book.

Traveling Libraries in Mongolia, Indonesia, Africa, and England

Author Margriet Ruurs was reading a newspaper when she saw a photograph showing a camel being used as a library in Kenya, Africa, to cart books from place to place. Says Ruurs, "Growing up in Holland, my father often took me to the library and I read many books. What if I hadn't had a library to depend upon? What if a camel was my library?" This idea sparked Ruurs to research different ways children get books in remote areas around the world. The result was her book *My Librarian Is a Camel.*

Typically people think of libraries as staying in one place, but that isn't always the case. Ruurs learned about another camel library in Mongolia, a wheelbarrow library along a beach in England, and a boat library in Indonesia. This story gave Ruurs an idea. "I started a way for people to collect and send books to these remote places. As I speak to kids in schools, I show images of these wondrous traveling libraries. Now these schools are starting to adopt traveling libraries in different countries. To prepare for collecting books, students study about the country and share information with others that promotes global literacy."

Libraries, whether in your neighborhood or on the back of a camel, provide opportunities to travel the world and learn about other people and places.

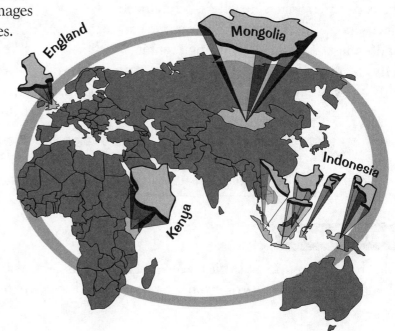

To find out more, read *My Librarian Is a Camel* by Margriet Ruurs (Boyds Mills Press, 2005). For information on adopting a traveling library, visit www.margrietruurs.com and click on "My Librarian Is a Camel." Then, click on "Adopt a Library."

Education for All—Including Girls—in Afghanistan

At age 6, Sadiqa Basiri fled the violence in Afghanistan with her parents and settled temporarily in Pakistan. As refugees they faced many challenges; however, Sadiqa and her sisters attended school, and her ability to receive an education changed her life forever.

At age 14, in 1994, Sadiqa visited Godah, her home village in eastern Afghanistan. She amazed the villagers with stories of how she had gone to school. The ruling Taliban, a very strict religious group, made it nearly impossible for girls to receive an education. Since 2001, restrictions have eased. Even so, more than a million school-age girls still do not attend school in Afghanistan.

As a young adult, Sadiqa returned to Godah in 2002 with a clear plan: to open a girls' school staffed by qualified teachers. Sadiqa and her two friends raised enough funds from previous jobs to pay for teachers, but they could not find any qualified women to teach. Determined, Sadiqa instead hired male teachers, convinced the townspeople of the importance of an education, and at last the Omid Learning Center was born. Through her efforts and the hard work of many, several girls' schools have been established across the country. Now, nearly 1,100 Afghan girls are attending school for the first time.

Read more about Sadiqa's experience in *Our Time Is Now* by Sheila Kinkade and Christine Macy (Pearson Foundation, 2005).

YOUR TURN

Did these international stories give you ideas for projects you can do in your community? What about global projects? Write your ideas here and discuss them with others.

Learning to Read & Write

You're reading this book and writing in it. But how did you learn to do that? Your parents and teachers probably had the greatest influence on your ability to learn to read and write. Answer the following questions. Then, consider the similarities and differences between you and other kids your age when it comes to literacy.

How did you learn to read? ....

What is your first memory of books? ....

Did someone in your family read aloud to you as a child? ....

When did you begin attending school? ....

How often do you go to a library? ....

What do you enjoy most about reading and writing? ....

....

For some people learning to read is easy, while for others it is a challenge. Think about your own experience learning to read. What challenges did you have? On your own or in small groups, come up with a list of ways learning to read can be challenging. Then brainstorm how each challenge can be overcome. The first few examples can help you get started.

> "Challenges can be stepping-stones or stumbling blocks."
> —Anonymous

Challenge of Learning to Read	How the Challenge Can Be Overcome
Lack of confidence	Read aloud to others who will provide support
Difficulty remembering what you read	Practice summarizing content, learn how to take notes
Unable to recognize big words	Use flashcards or word games to help improve vocabulary

TIME FOR REFLECTION

Turn to pages 37–38, and choose a reflection activity to complete.

Math & Computer Literacy

Literacy goes beyond reading and writing words. It also involves the ability to work with numbers and do simple tasks on a computer. Along with language skills, basic math and computer skills are an essential part of getting along in the world today.

Why is math so important? Well, it's *not* just about getting the right answers on an algebra test. Math is what you use to find out if you can catch the noon bus to the mall and make the 12:45 movie. The bus driver uses math when collecting fares. It is also the basis for operating the stoplights that keep the roads safe. Math is the hidden language behind nearly everything in the modern world.

Computers also are a big part of our lives. Many schools, companies, and governments around the world depend on computers. People use personal computers to do countless daily tasks such as find information on the Internet, write to family and friends, pay bills and taxes, and even shop for groceries. Having access to a computer and knowing how to use one is becoming a necessity.

In fact, both math and computer symbols are now a universal language. Can you match these symbols with what they represent?

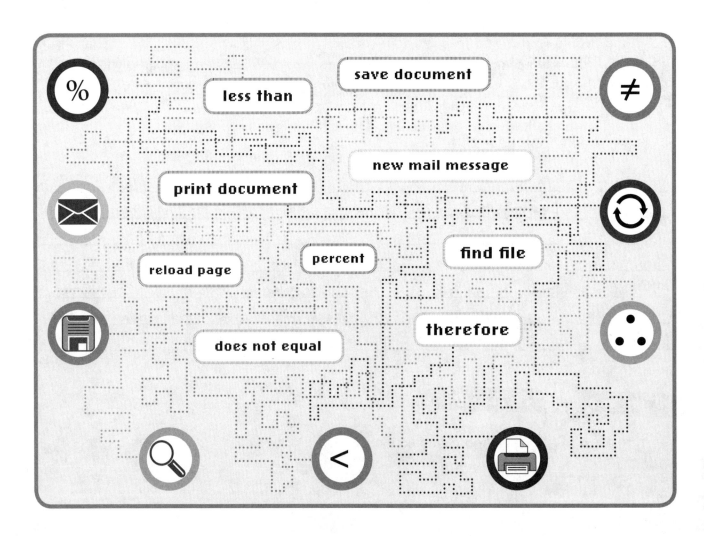

Can students help others strengthen their math and computer literacy? Absolutely. Just read the following examples.

Math Game Library

As part of a year-end project, middle school students at New Foundations Charter School in Pennsylvania were involved in creating a game to prepare students for their final exam in math. Each student chose a topic, developed a game, created all the pieces, and wrote a sheet with rules and instructions. They compiled all the games in a Math Game Library. Students used this library as a resource for extra help and to sharpen their skills throughout the year.

What would you add to a Math Game Library? Choose an idea from the following list or come up with your own. Create the game on your own or with a partner or small group. Decide if this game will be for kids in your grade or for younger kids.

Develop a special version of dominos or bingo that involves a math skill.

Take a popular card game and change the rules to include math.

Invent a new game using a checkerboard and playing pieces that are different geometric shapes.

Create a math game that also requires computer skills.

Kids for Computer Literacy

Many families in the rural community of Kansas, Oklahoma, did not have computers at home, and the town had no public library to provide them with computer access. What could middle school kids do to help? They decided to open their school's computer lab to local residents on Tuesday evenings and Saturday mornings. To prepare, the students learned how to use the computer résumé writing program and practiced creating and leading lessons to teach people how to use computers. After surveying the families to find out their interests, the students also located and bookmarked Web sites on the computers that contained information people wanted.

What could you do for people in your community who don't have access to computers?

Meet Kids in Action: Part 1

Every day kids improve their communities and our world. The stories in the "Meet Kids in Action" chapters of this book tell of kids who learn about literacy and contribute to their communities.

Ready, Set, Taxes!

Jolanda Burton, a tenth grader at St. Helena High in Greensburg, Louisiana, learned about doing tax returns in her math class. She thought of a way to help out in her rural community—offer free tax preparation for people in need. After getting additional training and tips from local tax accountants, Jolanda and her classmates were ready to go. In their desktop publishing class, they made advertisements for their services and posted them in businesses, community centers, and places of worship. When the time came, they set up tables at school with computers and tax software and provided free assistance and basic financial math tutoring to dozens of people. The students celebrated their accomplishment with a banquet attended by the people they had assisted. The project was so successful that people asked the students to do it again the following year.

Making Stories Personal

At Covington Middle School in Vancouver, Washington, eighth graders make special picture books. First, they interview second and third graders about their favorite activities, colors, pets, siblings, and interests. Then, they compose original stories that include one of the younger children in the role of a hero solving a problem. The student writers add information from their interviews with the children, and they make the stories interactive by including places where the reader predicts what happens next. The stories even include a blank page where children can draw or add their own endings. These personalized stories create enthusiastic young readers!

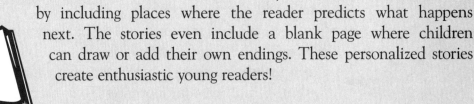

As you read these stories, do any ideas come to mind? Write them down as you read. Use them to start discussions and to help you take action.

Looking Back:
Historical Moments & Actions

In school you may have learned about times in history when people were not able to get books or attend school. Think of two historical events that made it challenging for people to get what they needed to learn and be literate.

When in history?	Who was affected?	What happened?

The First Public Library in America

In the 1730s, books were possessions of the wealthy, and few Americans had books in their homes. Benjamin Franklin was determined to change this. On July 1, 1731, Franklin and others signed an agreement to form a library in Philadelphia. People could become members by donating books and money. Every year, contributions helped build the collection and maintain the library. While the original collection consisted mostly of educational and religious books, soon topics included poetry, science, geography, exploration, and history. Even nonmembers could take books home, as long as they left something of value at the library that could be sold if they did not return the books.

From this single library in Philadelphia, the idea of public libraries spread to other cities. Now, over 16,500 public libraries exist in the United States.

> "Tell me and I forget. Teach me and I may remember. Involve me and I learn."
> —Benjamin Franklin, political leader, inventor, and author

YOUR TURN

Visit a nearby library to explore all the different kinds of information available. List three resources libraries have that you didn't already know about.

1.

2.

3.

Sequoyah: Creating a Written Language

W la
ma
na hna nah
qua

Today, about 6,800 languages exist in the world. Almost half are in danger of disappearing. Language does more than simply communicate a thought or message—it also preserves the culture of a people.

Sequoyah was born in eastern Tennessee in the 1760s, the son of a Cherokee mother and white father. He grew up to be a metalworker, but later, along with many Cherokees, he joined the U.S. Army to fight in the War of 1812 against Great Britain. Sequoyah noticed that he and the other Cherokees were not able to write letters to the people back home, read military orders, or write down events that happened like the other soldiers were able to do. This inspired Sequoyah to develop a way to capture the Cherokee language in writing. He created a symbol for each syllable of his language. These 85 symbols are still used today. In 1821, he presented his "syllabary" to the Cherokee Nation, and seven years later, the *Phoenix*, the first newspaper written in Cherokee, was published.

> To learn more, read *Sequoyah: The Cherokee Man Who Gave His People Writing* by James Rumford (Houghton Mifflin, 2004), a bilingual book in English and Cherokee.

Can you imagine creating a written language? What symbols would you use? Think of some words that would be important for people to be able to write down. Draw your symbols below.

Schools for Those in Need

Julius Rosenwald was the son of Jewish immigrants from Germany. A skillful leader and manager, he was president of the Sears department store company from 1908 to 1924. But Rosenwald wanted to do more than run a successful company—he wanted to make a difference.

While at Sears, Rosenwald met Dr. Booker T. Washington, an African-American leader, author, and educator, and the founder of the Tuskegee Institute in Alabama, a college for African-American students. The two men had great respect for one another. As a result, Washington convinced Rosenwald to help improve the education of African Americans in the rural southern United States where African-American students were not allowed to attend school with white children. What began as a project to create six schools grew into a project to construct over 5,000 schools, shops, and teachers' homes in 15 states. In each community where schools were built, Rosenwald used his business experience to help the local African-American community raise the needed money, purchase land and building supplies, and hire builders. Rosenwald donated $4.3 million in total and helped African-American communities raise more than $4.7 million.

> To learn more, read *Dear Mr. Rosenwald* by Carole B. Weatherford (Scholastic Press, 2006) and visit www.rosenwaldschools.com.

YOUR TURN

Mr. Rosenwald took action because he admired Booker T. Washington and what he had done for African-American students. Think of a person you admire who is involved in educating others. How could you take action to honor this person?

Making History Today

The previous examples of people helping others happened quite a while ago. But people are still taking action today to help others read and succeed, whether at the local, national, or international level. Read the following stories to find out how.

Demanding a School Budget

In Geneseo, New York, middle school students recently discovered their school district had not been given a budget for needed supplies in three years. They were outraged! They set out conducting interviews, going door-to-door with surveys, and doing in-depth research on the issue before finally making a presentation to the school board. Their speeches made quite an impression and the school board eventually approved a school budget with overwhelming public support. As a result, students saw a remarkable difference in the number of computers, textbooks, and other equipment available to them in their district—a difference that will be seen for years to come.

> Read more success stories about kids making lasting improvements to their schools and learn how you can, too, at www.youthactivism.com.

In Times of Disaster

Barbara Fenig, a high school junior at New York City's Calhoun School, made frequent visits to New Orleans, Louisiana, with her family. She was deeply upset by the disaster of Hurricane Katrina. Fenig learned of a school that had been badly damaged in the storm, and she also knew that many New Orleans schoolchildren had trouble reading and writing even before this tragedy. So she took action. "I decided to collect books because education is so important. We can avoid future disasters if people are educated—and the book drive was meant to help give all people access to education," Fenig says. She applied for and received money in the form of a Youth Leaders for Literacy Grant so she could pay to transport the books. She involved her entire school in helping. Over 2,000 books now fill the new shelves at St. Bernard's Parish School in Chalmette, a suburb of New Orleans.

> To learn more about Youth Leaders for Literacy Grants, visit www.nea.org/readacross/volunteer/index.html.

A Library Lost in War

In Basra, Iraq, Alia Muhammed Baker, head of the city's library, faced a serious problem. War was coming, so she asked the local government for help in moving the collection of nearly 70,000 books, many of them precious and rare. Government officials said they could not give Baker the help she needed, so she turned to others in her community. They helped her secretly move the books to nearby restaurants and shops for safekeeping. Their actions proved worthwhile—a short time after they had safely moved over 30,000 books, Basra's library was destroyed.

Baker made a commitment to build a new library. The American Library Association started a fund to provide books to the new Basra library and other libraries in need. Students in the United States heard Baker's story and raised money for the fund. As a result, the new Basra library now has more than 30,000 new books.

Iraq

Arabian Sea

To learn more, read *The Librarian of Basra: A True Story from Iraq* by Jeanette Winter (Harcourt Children's Books, 2005). For information about needed contributions, send an email to the American Library Association's International Relations Office: intl@ala.org.

YOUR TURN

Find out who keeps the libraries in good shape in your neighborhood. If there aren't any public libraries close to where you live, is there interest in creating one? How could you find out?

Learning from Reading:
Dear Whiskers

Books help give people a close-up view of situations they may not be familiar with. The book *Dear Whiskers* by Ann Whitehead Nagda offers a rare and accurate picture of an older child helping a younger child with literacy skills. This is often called "cross-age tutoring," an activity you might choose to do for service learning. Although *Dear Whiskers* is written for elementary school students, middle and high school students often read this book to prepare to teach reading to younger students or to adults who have literacy difficulties or who are just learning English.

If you are working in a large group, form groups of four to read and discuss the *Dear Whiskers* excerpt on pages 22–23. Assign each person in the group one of the "connector" roles below. Each connector's job is to lead a group discussion about the story from a specific point of view. He or she asks the questions listed (along with others that come to mind) and encourages group members to respond. Choose one person to read the story aloud to the rest of the group. Feel free to write notes and ideas in the Literature Circle on the following page. If you are working alone, consider the questions under each connector and give your own answers.

Personal Connector:
Ask questions that connect the story to group members' experiences, such as:
1. Do any characters remind you of people you know? How?
2. Have you been in situations similar to what is described in the book? What happened?
3. How have you or people you know resolved similar situations?

Literary Connector:
Ask questions that connect this story to other stories group members have read, such as:
1. Which characters remind you of characters from other stories? Why?
2. What situations are similar to what happens in other stories?
3. What might Jenny say about these other characters or situations?

Service Connector:
Ask questions that connect this story to ideas for service projects, such as:
1. What needs to be fixed in this situation?
2. Did any characters in this story participate in service activities?
3. What service ideas did you think of when you read this story?

School Connector:
Ask questions that connect this story to your school, such as:
1. What were the school experiences of characters in this story?
2. What ideas in this story have you learned about or experienced in school?
3. What do you think other people your age would learn by reading this story?

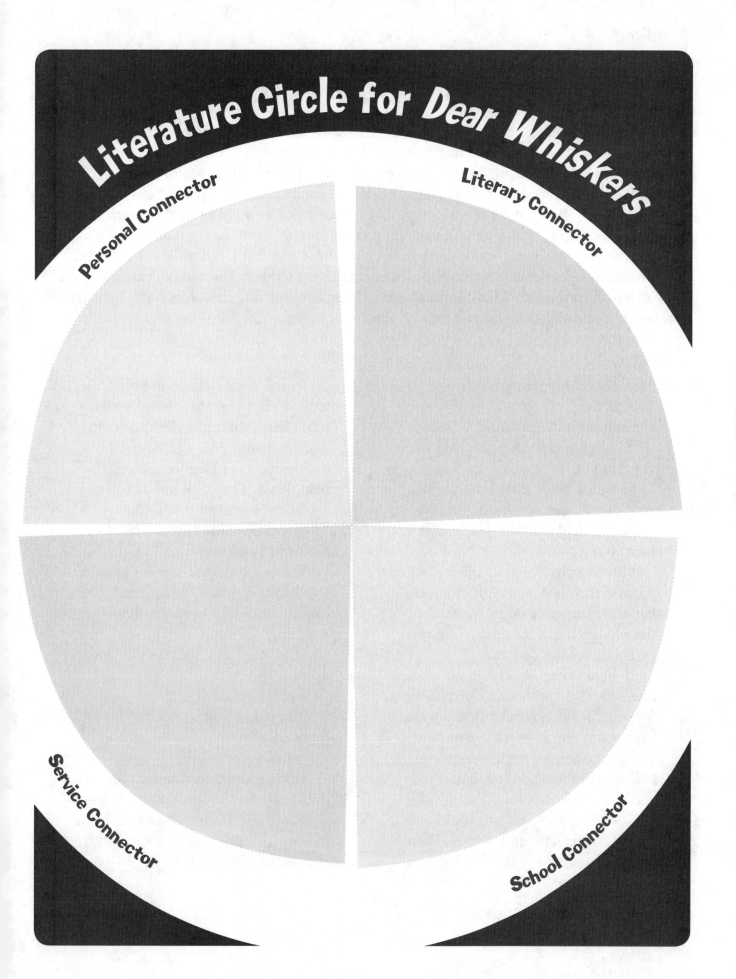

Literature Circle for *Dear Whiskers*

Personal Connector

Literary Connector

Service Connector

School Connector

An Excerpt from *Dear Whiskers*

The story *Dear Whiskers* is about Jenny, a fourth grader, who is a tutor and pen pal to a second grader in her school named Sameera. Jenny's first assignment is to write letters to Sameera as if she were a mouse living in the younger girl's desk. This seems silly to Jenny. Her teacher explains, "We want to give the second graders lots of practice reading." Jenny signs her first letter "Whiskers" and waits for a letter back. But Sameera is a new girl from Saudi Arabia, who barely speaks English. Jenny wants a different pen pal! Instead, Jenny has a challenge with added responsibilities—not just a young pen pal, but also one whose first language is not English.

In the following scene from the book, Sameera has just left her class without permission and is walking down the school hall. Jenny is sent to bring her back and try reading with her, and so she meets Sameera face-to-face for the first time.

"Sameera, I'm Jenny. I'm supposed to read to you."

Sameera stared at Jenny.

"Come," said Jenny. She held out her hand.

Sameera held Jenny's hand. She didn't smile, but she didn't run away. Jenny felt relieved. She led Sameera back to the classroom.

Miss Murphy looked up when Jenny entered the classroom with Sameera, but then turned back to the student she was helping. Jenny guessed she was on her own with Sameera.

"I have some books," Jenny said. She still had the books clutched in her other hand. She held them out for Sameera to see. Sameera looked away.

"Where can we read?" asked Jenny as she looked around the room. A red-and-blue plaid couch stood against the wall. Jenny led Sameera to the couch and sat down. Sameera hesitated. Then she sat down, too.

Jenny opened the first book. She took a deep breath and started to read. She pointed to the mouse and said his name. Jenny tilted the book so Sameera could see the picture. She read slowly. The book had some hard words. She stumbled on the words "pebble path." She had to sound out the word "quivering."

When Jenny read the last page of the book, she said, "The end." She closed the book. Sameera didn't say anything.

"Did you like the book?" Jenny asked.

Sameera nodded.

"Should I read another book?" Jenny asked.

Sameera shrugged.

Jenny guessed that meant Sameera didn't care one way or another. At least she sat on the couch and listened. Well, maybe she wasn't listening, but at least she sat still. She didn't leave the room.

Jenny looked over at Miss Murphy. Miss Murphy looked up and smiled at her and nodded her head. Jenny figured the teacher was encouraging her to go ahead and read more. She opened the second book. It was about a mouse who ate a cookie. When she said the word "cookie," Jenny pretended she was eating a cookie and said, "Yum, yum."

Sameera grinned.

Jenny smiled back. It was the first time she had seen Sameera look happy. She read on. Sameera didn't grin again, but she held one side of the book and seemed to be paying attention.

The recess bell rang. All the kids rushed for their coats.

Jenny was in the middle of reading the last page of the book.

Sameera jumped up. Without a backward look, she rushed to get her coat and left the room.

Jenny watched her go.

The Story Behind *Dear Whiskers:* An Interview with Author Ann Whitehead Nagda

"My daughter Asha's fifth-grade teacher paired her class with second graders for a letter-writing exchange. Asha had to write letters to her second-grade pen pal pretending to be a mouse named Whiskers. This idea formed the original centerpiece of *Dear Whiskers,*" says author Ann Whitehead Nagda. "Then I met a young girl from Saudi Arabia named Aroa who was struggling in elementary school; she became the model for Sameera.

"I hope readers see that going out of their way for people who are struggling or who have different backgrounds can enrich their lives, that being kind is important. Getting involved isn't always easy. Jenny is so frustrated she asks for another pen pal who isn't so much trouble! With teacher encouragement, Jenny makes a breakthrough with Sameera and feels better about herself and her abilities.

"I heard that a high school in Ohio had every ninth grader read *Dear Whiskers* as their first class text. My book helped prepare these students to be tutors to elementary children. You never know who might be moved or changed by a story!"

YOUR TURN

How do you think Jenny felt when Sameera jumped up to leave? How do you think Sameera felt? Should Jenny keep tutoring Sameera? How do you think this book will end?

Cross-Age Tutoring & Helping English Language Learners

Imagine that, as a service project, you are going to help a younger child read a book. You will tutor the child (the tutee) four times for 45 minutes each time. You know the tutee has some basic reading skills but doesn't seem interested in trying to improve. By yourself, with a partner, or in a small group, do the following:

List three ways you could prepare for the first tutoring session:

1. ....

2. ....

3. ....

Identify three things you might ask for help with between sessions:

1. ....

2. ....

3. ....

Describe three benefits for each of the following people:

You (the tutor)

1. .... 2. .... 3. ....

Your tutee

1. .... 2. .... 3. ....

Your tutee's teacher

1. .... 2. .... 3. ....

Being a Great Cross-Age Tutor

How can you learn to be an effective tutor? Read the following list of tips. If you're working in a large group, form smaller groups. Each group can take one or two tips and prepare a brief demonstration to teach the tips to others.

 Gather your favorite children's books from home or the library, or ask a librarian for age-appropriate book suggestions. Think about what makes a story interesting to a child. Practice reading the books aloud to yourself, in pairs, or in small groups.

 Get to know your tutee by asking questions about his or her interests, skills, and talents. Talk with the child about the importance of getting to know each other to build trust and to find books she or he will like.

 Design action-packed activities to help children learn the alphabet, punctuation, or other literacy skills. For example, you could use chalk to outline letters on pavement and have students walk the shapes. Simple stretches can also help the child settle down.

 Teach listening skills by reading a paragraph aloud and asking the child to tell you a summary of it. This activity is a good idea for every tutoring session.

 Help your tutee remember what he or she read by using reflection. Ask the child to complete these phrases: "Today I learned . . ." or "I want to remember . . ." Write down the responses and review them at the next session. Include them in a little book of accomplishments to give the child when tutoring ends.

 Do service learning together! Work with your tutee on alphabet books, write stories or poetry, make a comic book, or design a bookmark about a favorite story. You can give these to the child's class or school library, or the child can exchange them with other students.

Participate in a global bookmark exchange at the Web site of author Margriet Ruurs: www.margrietruurs.com. Click on "A Book Marks Our World."

Helping English Language Learners

Like Sameera from the *Dear Whiskers* story, many adults and children in the United States have moved here from another country where the first language they learned was not English. Most of these new immigrants choose to learn English as a second language so they can participate fully in American society. However, they will tell you that learning a second language is *not* easy!

Imagine you are tutoring an adult who is learning English as a second language. How would you change the tips you just read about to help her or him? What practical skills could you emphasize with this kind of tutoring? Describe how you would use the following items when providing assistance to English language learners.

phone book	
restaurant menu	
street map	
job résumé	
newspaper	

List two more items you might use, and how they would be helpful.

....

....

Turn to pages 37–38, and choose a reflection activity to complete.

Meet Kids in Action: Part 2

Making Sense of Sayings

Maybe you've heard the phrase, "Don't let the cat out of the bag!" It means, don't give away a secret. This saying is called an idiom—a phrase that doesn't mean exactly what it says. You may know what this phrase means, but if English is your second language, idioms can be hard to understand. In West Hollywood, California, English speakers partnered with Russian-born students to make a book that helped explain idioms through pictures and words. Each pair of students took a specific idiom and discussed what people might think it means and what it *really* means. The students also made two illustrations to accompany the description of their idiom. For example, the first picture for "Don't let the cat out of the bag!" showed a cat hiding in a sack, and the second picture showed a child saying, "Shh!" The students put all the pictures and explanations into a workbook to be used by new students of English.

A Book Buddy Club

A take-charge group of middle school students at The Stadium School in Baltimore, Maryland, formed the Youth Dreamers to make their dreams a reality. They developed a Saturday Book Buddy Club with money they received from the Youth Leaders for Literacy program. The book club was for families and consisted of six one-hour meetings to get kids and their parents reading together. Book club members read the novel *Stargirl* by Jerry Spinelli. The money paid for book copies for each family and comfortable pillows to sit on. The students planned activities for each meeting, such as read-alouds from the novel and group discussions that centered on peer pressure, a main theme of the book. At the final gathering, parents and kids gave a variety of presentations. For example, one group did a news report and interviewed characters from the book.

To learn more about the Youth Dreamers' projects, visit www.youthdreamers.org.

Writing Your Own ABCs

When eighth grader Devora Kaye saw a need for a book, she wrote one. In fact, she developed an easy design that has been used to create alphabet books on many different topics. All during high school, she traveled throughout the United States teaching adults and kids about the importance of books and how to use her design to write books for others. As a service project, what kind of ABC book could you write?

Before you begin, consider the following questions and write your responses.

Why do we have books?

Where do we find books?

What different kinds of books are there?

Where could you donate books? (Add to the following ideas.)

• Maternity wards (include a letter you write titled "Why it is important to read to your child")

• Waiting rooms in ....

• ....

• ....

• ....

How to Make Your ABC Book

You will need several sheets of unlined white paper, a pencil, and a black pen. Black ink shows up better when you make copies. It also allows the kids who receive your book to add color!

Step 1: Decide on a topic for your ABC book. For example, the ABCs of Friendship.

Step 2: If you're working in a group, divide into pairs. Each pair takes one alphabet letter at a time until all 26 letters have been used.

Step 3: Brainstorm word ideas for your letter that relate to the topic. For example, if your topic is friendship and you have the letter "B," you might come up with words like *best* or *buddy*.

Step 4: Brainstorm picture ideas that relate to your word. For example, if your word is *buddy*, you might draw two friends holding hands.

Step 5: Create your page using the design below. Use white paper and black ink. Be sure to check spelling and punctuation.

Step 6: Place your page in the ABC book in alphabetical order. You may want to include a cover, a title page, an "about this book" section, and an "about the author(s)" page.

Step 7: Make photocopies of your finished book, staple each copy together, and pass them out to places that could use them.

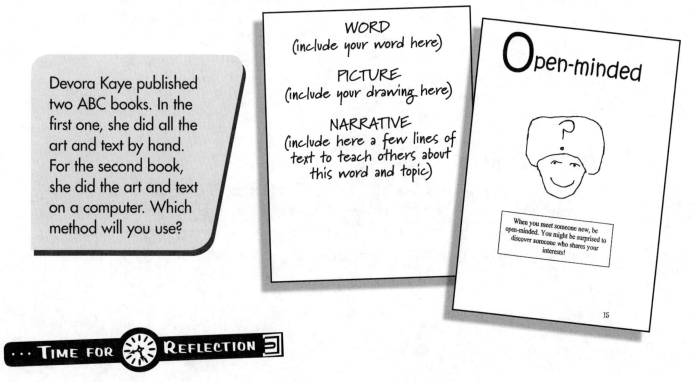

Devora Kaye published two ABC books. In the first one, she did all the art and text by hand. For the second book, she did the art and text on a computer. Which method will you use?

WORD
(include your word here)

PICTURE
(include your drawing here)

NARRATIVE
(include here a few lines of text to teach others about this word and topic)

Open-minded

When you meet someone new, be open-minded. You might be surprised to discover someone who shares your interests!

15

···TIME FOR REFLECTION ∃

Turn to pages 37–38, and choose a reflection activity to complete.

Getting Started:
What Does Your Community Need?

The kids you've read about in this workbook based their projects on real community needs. Now it's your turn to find out the needs in your community so you can make a plan for action.

Use the questions in the following four categories as guides for learning more about literacy in your area. If you're working in a large group, form four smaller groups, with each group focusing on one category and gathering information in a different way.

Media

What media (newspapers, TV stations, Web sites) in your community might have helpful information for you? List ways you can work with different media to learn about literacy issues in your community.

Interviews

Think of a person who is knowledgeable about literacy in your area—perhaps someone who works at a service agency, a government office, or a school, or someone who has personally struggled with reading or writing. Write questions you would ask this person in an interview.

Surveys

A survey can help you find out what people know about literacy and get ideas for helping. Who could you survey—students, family members, neighbors? How many surveys would you want to have completed? Write three survey questions.

Who to survey: How many surveys:

Questions for the survey:

1.

2.

3.

Observation and Experience

What ways are there to gather information through your own observation and experience? Where would you go? What would you do there? How would you keep track of what you find out?

Next Step: Share your ideas. Make a plan for gathering information in the four ways just discussed. If you are working in small groups, each group may want to involve people in other groups. For example, everyone could help conduct the survey and collect the results. Record the information you learn in the next chapter, "Our Community Needs."

Turn to pages 37–38, and choose a reflection activity to complete.

Our Community Needs
What I Learned From . . .

 Media:

 Interviews:

 Surveys:

 Observation and Experience:

As a result of your investigation, what do you think are the most important needs in your community involving literacy?

Which method of gathering information did you like best? Why?

Taking Action

This is your tool to begin making plans for action. (If you are in a large group, work together in small groups on this task.) Start by selecting the community you want to help. Your school? Your neighborhood? The whole country? People around the globe? Then, go to Step 1.

 Step 1: Think about the needs in your community involving literacy. Make a list.

 Step 2: Identify what you already know. Select one community need from your list:

- What is the cause?

- Who is helping?

 Step 3: Find out more.

- What else do we want to know about this community need and the ways we can help?

- How can we find out what we want to know?

 Step 4: Plan for action.

- To help our community, we will:

- To make this happen, we will take on these responsibilities:

Who	will do what	by when?	Resources needed

Service Learning Proposal

Use the information from the previous "Taking Action" chapter to develop a written proposal of your plan. You can give this proposal to others in your school or organization and to other people or groups that plan to work with you.

Student names: ....

Teacher/Adult leader: ....

School/Organization: ....

Address: ....

Phone: .... Fax: .... Email: ....

Project name: ....

Need—Why this plan is needed:

Purpose—How this plan will help:

Participation—Who will help, and what they will do:

    Students: ....

    Teachers: ....

    Other adults: ....

    Organizations or groups: ....

Outcomes—What we expect to happen as the result of our work:

How we will check outcomes—What evidence we will collect and how we will use it:

Resources—What we need to get the job done, such as supplies:

Signatures:

Project Promotion:
Finding Resources & Telling Your Story

Now that you have an action plan and a proposal, you are ready to promote your project. Write ways you can do so in each category listed below. In the Follow-Up section, decide who will do what needs to be done. If you are working in a large group, form six smaller groups and have each group focus on a category. After you come up with ideas for your category, present your suggestions.

Donations: What is needed for your project (such as flyers, T-shirts, or food)? Who might donate items?

Fund-raising ideas and resources: Be creative and invite community support.

Evidence: Chart your progress for others to see.

Media madness: Press releases, radio spots, cable access TV, Web sites—get the word out!

Presentation opportunities: Consider school and community events, like council meetings.

Partners in the community: Brainstorm all possible partners—even unusual ones.

Follow-Up
Roles and responsibilities: Who will do what?

Turn to pages 37–38, and choose a reflection activity to complete.

Make Your Action Memorable

As you put your plan into action, use this page as a scrapbook to record what happens. Add art and photos or glue in a newspaper article.

What happened today?

 Any new bright ideas to help the project be even better?

One page may not be enough. You may want to keep your own service learning journal in a notebook or start a large scrapbook for the entire group to use.

 Capture the moment! Add a photo or drawing of what you did or saw.

Pause, Look Back, & Reflect

Do you sometimes press the pause button on a remote control? Reflection is like that—a chance to pause and think about your experience from many angles. Sometimes the action in service learning occurs on one day, sometimes it extends over weeks or months. No matter how long your service learning lasts, these pages will help you reflect on what you've done. Write the date next to each reflection activity to help you remember the sequence you followed to pause, look back, and reflect.

Date:

What was special about today's activity? How did you make a difference?

Date:

What new things have you discovered about yourself through this experience?

Date:

Consider this quote: "If you can't make a mistake, you can't make anything," by educator Marva Collins. What mistakes have led to new ideas and improvements to your project?

Date:

If you were writing a book about your service learning experience, what would the cover look like and what would the first page say?

Date:

Close your eyes and think about the word *literacy*. What images come to mind? Repeat with the word *illiterate*. Share your thoughts with others. Combine words with images to create a visual representation of literacy.

Once You Know It, Show It!

You've put your plan into action and seen the results. Now it's time for demonstration—the stage where you show others what you've learned about literacy, how you learned it, and what you've contributed to your community. This demonstration of your service learning can take any form you like: a letter, article, video, pamphlet, artistic display, performance, or PowerPoint presentation.

To help you make the most of your demonstration, answer these questions:

Who is your audience?

What do you most want to tell them about what you've learned?

What do you most want to tell them about how you provided service?

Are there any community partners who you might like to participate in the demonstration?

What form of demonstration would you like to use?

On a separate sheet of paper, write your plan for demonstration.

If you are part of a class or youth group, share your ideas for demonstration with the others you're working with. How can you best use each person's talents and skills as part of your demonstration?

What You've Learned & Accomplished

Take time to think about what you have learned, the service you provided, and the process you used—how you made everything happen. On your own, answer the following questions. Discuss your responses with the people involved in your service learning project.

Learning

What information did you learn in preparing to do service?

What skills did you develop through the activities?

How did this project help you better understand literacy?

What did you learn about yourself?

What did you learn about working with others?

What did you learn about your community?

How will you use what you learned in this experience?

Service

What was the need met by your service project?

What contribution did you make?

How did your service affect the community?

Process

How did you help with project planning?

What decisions did you make? How did you solve problems?

What differences were there between your project proposal and what actually happened?

What ideas do you have for improving any part of your project?

What do you think is the best part about service learning? Why?

What's Next?

Congratulations! You have completed this service learning workbook on literacy. However, this is only the beginning. You may want to find ways to stay actively involved with helping in your community. This final activity will help you determine what's next.

Write a few sentences about what you would like to see happen in your community.

What ideas in this workbook can you use to help make your community a better place?

On each step, write one thing you can do to stay involved in service.

FYI (For Your Information)

The Internet

America's Literacy Directory is part of the National Institute for Literacy and Partners. Find literacy programs, volunteer opportunities, and contacts in your area. Visit www.literacy directory.org.

bridges4kids is an organization that helps families, schools, and communities work together to solve problems. Its literacy page links to articles, as well as to other Web sites and resource ideas. Check out www.bridges4kids.org.

The National Institute for Literacy LINCS (Literacy Information and Communication System) is devoted to adult and family literacy. The Web site contains facts and statistics, mentions of literacy in the news, and many other resources. Go to www.nifl.gov/lincs.

The Bookshelf

Fahrenheit 451 by Ray Bradbury (Simon & Schuster, 1953/1993). Guy Montag and his fellow firemen are paid to burn books. He never questions this job until he meets Clarisse, a girl who changes his outlook. One day he saves a book from the fires, hoping to find answers within it. Instead, he is taken on a remarkable journey of self-discovery. Fiction, 208 pages.

The Kid's Guide to Social Action: How to Solve the Social Problems You Choose—and Turn Creative Thinking into Positive Action by Barbara A. Lewis (Free Spirit Publishing, 1998). Exciting, empowering, and packed with information, this is the ultimate guide for kids who want to make a difference in the world. Learn how to write letters, do interviews, make speeches, take surveys, raise funds, get media coverage, and more. Nonfiction, 224 pages.

Learning Disabilities by Christina M. Girod (Lucent Books, 2001). This book provides a wide-reaching overview of learning disabilities that is useful for students who are tutoring or doing other service learning projects involving kids or adults with learning disabilities. Nonfiction, 96 pages.

A Life Like Mine: How Children Live Around the World (DK Publishing and UNICEF, 2002). Through amazing photographs, meet children from around the globe and visit 180 countries. One topic explored is *development*, which includes the right to an education. See how children attend school in many parts of the world. Nonfiction, 128 pages.

The Strength of Saints by A. LaFaye (Simon & Schuster, 2002). It is 1936, and teenager Nissa Bergen has a mind of her own. She is the librarian in a small southern town that segregates people based on race. She believes that's wrong and wants to unite the community. Doing what's right may not be easy, but Nissa is up to the challenge. Fiction, 192 pages.

A Note to Teachers, Youth Leaders, Parents, & Other Adults:
How to Use This Workbook

Young people have ideas, energy, and enthusiasm that can benefit our communities once they get involved. The question may be, where to start? By giving this book to students or to your own children, you are helping them participate successfully in service learning. The process of completing the activities helps them develop personal skills, knowledge, and abilities required to address the community needs they care about. Kids can use this workbook themselves, or adults can guide them in its use in school, youth groups, or a family setting. The following sections explain in more detail how these groups can get the most out of this workbook.

In a School Setting

This book can easily be used in various ways within a school:

Academic Class: As part of a unit of study about literacy, whether local, national, or international, this book provides an interdisciplinary approach to examining this important issue. Students look at civic issues, analyze and compare statistics, read and discuss selections of fiction and nonfiction, develop activity plans, and put their plans into action. The series of lessons can be implemented over three to six weeks of class time when used continuously, depending on the length of the service project. Another option is to complete one to two activities per week and extend the study over a semester.

Advisory Class: Many schools have a dedicated 30- to 40-minute weekly advisory class meant to improve academic skills, provide opportunities for social-emotional development, and allow for a successful experience in a course of study or exploration. This book allows students to develop communication and research skills, teamwork, and problem solving, while working to make a significant contribution. When implemented in a weekly advisory class, all the activities could be completed in about three months.

After-School Program: These varied activities suit an after-school program. The lessons are easily implemented and include many creative opportunities for expression that vary the teaching and learning methods. Different ages of students also can collaborate successfully. Activities include partner work as well as small and large group experiences. If implemented twice a week in an after-school program, the lessons would most likely extend over three months.

Student Council: If you are looking for a way to transform a typical student council community service project into service learning, this book can be your guide. As students are exploring the issues, they can develop a project that extends into the student body. Part of the project could be an awareness campaign with the leadership students sharing with fellow students what they consider to be the most important information in this book, augmented by what they discover through research.

In Youth Groups

As service learning grows in popularity with youth groups, program staff often looks for activities that encourage academic skills in a nontraditional manner. Use of this workbook is most effective when consistent—for example, one or two times per week—so students know what to expect and what is expected of them. The activities compiled here offer opportunities for lively discussion, firsthand community experiences, creative expression (for example, writing, poetry, drama, and art), and integrated reflection.

As a Family

Family service projects provide opportunities for common exploration and experience. Rather than emphasizing the academic elements, families can use the workbook to guide them through the terrain of the service learning process while gaining collective knowledge and stimulating ideas for projects. It's helpful for family members to approach the topic of literacy on equal ground, with the youngest members being encouraged to share their thoughts and ideas.

For every participant, this book is designed to open minds, create possibilities, and encourage the lasting benefits that occur when making a contribution of one's personal talents and skills. Each person has value in the service learning process.

Cathryn Berger Kaye, M.A.

Sources for Literacy Facts

Pages 3–6: Statistics in the chapter "Service + Learning = Service Learning" are from "Children and Television FAQ" Center for Media Education; "Television and Health," The Sourcebook for Teaching Science (www.csun.edu/~vceed002/health/docs/tv&health.html, accessed December 10, 2006); and "TV-Turnoff Network," Center for Screen-Time Awareness (www.tvturnoff.org, accessed December 10, 2006); and "Leaving Boys Behind: Public High School Graduation Rates," *Civic Report No. 48 April 2006* (Manhattan Institute for Policy Research, www.manhattan-institute.org/html/cr_48.htm, accessed January 9, 2007).

Page 7: Statistics in the chapter "Getting the Facts About Literacy" are from *A Life Like Mine: How Children Live Around the World* (New York: UNICEF and DK Publishing, 2002); "International Literacy Day," International Reading Association (www.reading.org/association/meetings/literacy_day.html, accessed December 10, 2006); and "Mapping the Global Literacy Challenge," *Education for All Global Monitoring Report 2006* (United Nations Educational, Scientific and Cultural Organization, www.unesco.org/education, accessed December 10, 2006).

Pages 15–17: Statistics in the chapter "Looking Back: Historical Moments & Actions" are from "Library Fact Sheet 1," September 2005, American Library Association (www.ala.org/ala/alalibrary/libraryfactsheet, accessed January 12, 2007); The Rosenwald Schools Initiative (www.rosenwaldschools.com, accessed August 29, 2006); and "Author's Note" from *Dear Mr. Rosenwald* by Carole B. Weatherford (New York: Scholastic, 2006).